One Hundred Houses

by Steven Otfinoski

MODERN CURRICULUM PRESS

Pearson Learning Group

In the summer of 1998, hundreds of people across America came to Houston, Texas. They came to build houses—one hundred of them. Many of these folks spent their summer vacations banging hammers and laying roofs in the hot sun.

These people were volunteers. They were working for Habitat for Humanity. It is a group that builds homes for needy people. Habitat for Humanity International was organized in 1976. Since then, it has built houses for people all around the world.

But Habitat for Humanity is not a charity. Anyone who applies for a home must be willing to work for it. Homeowners work alongside volunteers. Together, they get the job done.

"It's been a great experience," says Betty Polk. "It's hard work. But it's been fun. And every drop of sweat is worth it." Betty and her husband Seff put in 300 hours of work.

The people who donate their time and skills come from many backgrounds. Some are construction workers. Some are office workers. There is even a former president among them.

He is Jimmy Carter. He has been volunteering for the group since 1984. Carter led the Houston project. It was the group's largest project in the United States.

"It's fulfilling," Carter says. "It's a wonderful experience for us. There's such a bonding between the house owner and the people who work on the home."

7

Another volunteer is Greg Janson. When he's not building houses for Habitat for Humanity, Greg is an accountant. He had a great time on a work project in 1997. When he got home, he called his mother. "You have got to come with me," he advised her.

After that, Joanne Janson worked with her son. She loved it too. Now she is looking forward to the next project.

Cathy Keating also enjoys working for Habitat for Humanity. She finds it a nice change. Back home in Oklahoma, her husband is the governor.

"I think all you have to do is be involved once. Then you catch the fever," she says. "There's a place for everybody. Whether you're young or old, skilled or unskilled, there's something for everybody to do to be a part of the team."

Habitat for Humanity is organized around a volunteer work force. Some volunteers sign up people for work crews. Others cook and serve meals and snacks for the hungry workers. Doctors and nurses volunteer too. They care for anyone injured on the job.

Some volunteers are on the Green Team. Their job is to pick up garbage and other goods for recycling. Crews are also advised by the Green Team on ways to save energy.

The new houses are built
to last. Flooring is put in. Doors
are hung. Painting crews are
organized. Sometimes businesses
donate wood.

Volunteers even plant grass
and trees in the yards.

Finally all the work is done.
Each house is then dedicated. It is
a thrilling moment for volunteers
and homeowners alike. Everyone
takes pride in a job well done.

Building houses is not Habitat for Humanity's only goal. They also help people take pride in their work. They help them to feel part of a community too.

"I've learned so much. I could go out there and build me another little home," says Betty Polk. Many of the homeowners do just that. They want to help build someone else's dream home.

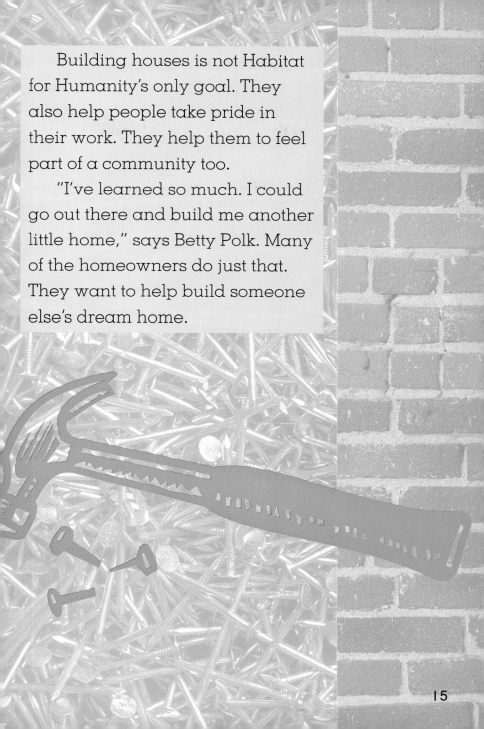

Olga Martinez has a Habitat for Humanity house. She is happy to have a home for her three children.

But for her, it doesn't end there. "Next year," she promises, "when someone needs help, I'm going to be there."